Dale Earnhardt, Jr.

Born to Race

Dale Earnhardt, Jr.

Born to Race

Ken Garfield

Enslow Publishers, Inc.

40 Industrial Road   PO Box 38
Box 398   Aldershot
Berkeley Heights, NJ 07922   Hants GU12 6BP
USA   UK
http://www.enslow.com

Library of Congress Cataloging-in-Publication Data

Garfield, Ken.
    Dale Earnhardt, Jr. : born to race / Ken Garfield.
       p. cm. — (Sports leaders)
    Includes bibliographical references and index.
    ISBN 0-7660-2424-5
    1. Earnhardt, Dale, Jr.—Juvenile literature. 2. Automobile racing drivers—
United States—Biography—Juvenile literature. I. Title. II. Sports leaders series.
    GV1032.E19G37   2005
    796.72'092—dc22

                                          2004026103

Printed in the United States of America

10 9 8 7 6 5 4 3 2 1

To Our Readers:
We have done our best to make sure all Internet Addresses in this book were active and
appropriate when we went to press. However, the author and the publisher have no con-
trol over and assume no liability for the material available on those Internet sites or on
other Web sites they may link to. Any comments or suggestions can be sent by e-mail to
comments@enslow.com or to the address on the back cover.

Illustration Credits: AP/Wide World Photos.

Cover Illustration: AP/Wide World Photos.

CONTENTS

DALE

To understand the amazing popularity of the National Association of Stock Car Auto Racing (NASCAR) and the First Family of the sport, all you have to do is say one word: Dale.

Whether you are referring to the father or his son, you are talking about two race car drivers whose daring, courage, and skill are so great, they only need one name to be recognized by sports fans the world over.

In a recent survey of fans by *Sports Illustrated* magazine, Dale Earnhardt, Sr., was named the best driver ever in NASCAR history by 56 percent of the fans polled. Finishing a distant second was Richard Petty, with 17 percent.[1]

And in the race for favorite current NASCAR driver, Dale Earnhardt, Jr., was chosen by 28 percent, far ahead of the 15 percent of second-place finisher Jeff Gordon. In the race for which driver sells the most toy cars, caps, and other souvenirs displaying his name and race car number, it is no contest: Dale Jr.[2]

And all that came Dale Jr.'s way even before he won the famed Daytona 500—the Super Bowl of NASCAR—for the first time to open the 2004 season on February 15, 2004.

"I don't think you can put your arms around the total impact the Earnhardts have had on NASCAR and racing in general," said Jerry Gappens, who helps handle publicity for Lowe's Motor Speedway near Charlotte, North Carolina.[3]

Who are these two great athletes who have helped make NASCAR second only to the National Football League (NFL) in TV ratings and able to draw more than one hundred thousand fans to tracks around the country?

Dale Earnhardt, Sr., was a NASCAR legend, a small-town kid from Kannapolis, North Carolina, who grew up to represent everything that's great about the sport—talent, drive, determination, and a devotion to the sport, his family, and his fans.

Dale died at age forty-nine in a final-lap crash, when his car slammed into the concrete wall at the Daytona 500 on February 18, 2001, at Daytona Beach, Florida. Millions of fans were shocked as they watched him lose his life in the most famous NASCAR race of all, doing what he did better than just anybody in the history of the sport: racing hard and fast to the finish line.

No wonder everyone knew him as The Intimidator, which meant he struck fear in other drivers' hearts when they saw him in their rearview mirror.

Dale won 76 Winston Cup races (the series is now known as the Nextel Cup, named for the communications company that sponsors it) and 7 season championships. That means in each of those seven seasons, he won more points during all the races combined than any other driver, even if he did not cross the finish line first. The idea is to run as close to the front as you can for as many laps as you can. That is consistency.

Beyond his victories, Dale left behind a lot of memories of his famous black No. 3 Chevrolet Monte Carlo. Anywhere you go in the United States,

Dale Earnhardt, Jr., (8) passes Tony Stewart (20) in the final laps of the Daytona 500 on February 15, 2004.

you will find racing fans proudly wearing black ball caps with his famous No. 3. At the start of races now, many of his fans will stand and hold up three fingers on Lap 3, another sign of their love and respect.

These days, though, race fans are also wearing the red No. 8 cap that is being made famous by the other superstar driver named Dale—Dale Earnhardt, Jr. The son of a legend, Dale Jr. has not reached the success his father attained. Yet.

Born October 10, 1974, he grew up around racing and joined NASCAR's top circuit full-time in 2000, when he started off driving for a team owned by his dad. Since then, Junior, or Little E as he is known in the sport, has won nine races through the 2003 season. He finished third in the points standings in 2003—good, but not quite as great as his father's record.

What makes father and son so popular? Gappens said fans were drawn to Dale Earnhardt's simple country roots. He worked hard for everything he had. And when he got on the track, he seemed to have more courage than just about anyone, racing his car into the corners and within inches of the bumper of the car in front of his. All that made him super-popular with the farmers, factory workers, and other

Dale Earnhardt, Jr., and his crew celebrate their victory at the 2004 Daytona 500.

down-to-earth people who flock to the races. Plus he never got too big to sign an autograph, go hunting, or work on the family farm.

"I think people can relate to that," Gappens said, adding that people who work hard for a living save their Sundays to follow one of their own. "People need something to cheer for every day of their lives."[4]

When Dale Sr. died at Daytona, they turned their cheers to Dale Jr. because he was carrying on the famous family name. Gappens has heard people say it many times at the track: "I'm pulling for Junior because I liked his dad and his grandfather."[5]

Dale Jr. has been able to please all the older fans of his father while attracting new, younger fans to NASCAR, and girls, who are drawn to his good looks. He is not bashful about telling people he enjoys a good party with his buddies. He shops at Wal-Mart. He has not gotten too big or conceited. He wears his pants baggy and his cap on backward, just like other young people his age. He has been on the cover of *TV Guide* and many other magazines, and appeared in an MTV video. He even made *People* magazine's 2004 list of "Most Beautiful People," with all the movie and TV stars.

★ ★ ★ ★ ★ ★ ★ ★ ★ ★ ★ ★ ★ ★ ★ ★

GETTING TO KNOW
DALE EARNHARDT, JR.

Born: October 10, 1974.

Residence: Mooresville, North Carolina.

Height: 6 feet.

Weight: 170 lbs.

Nickname: Little E.

Hero: His dad, the late Dale Earnhardt, Sr.

Favorite movies: *Cast Away* and *Saving Private Ryan*.

Favorite vacation spots: Hawaii or Jamaica.

Favorite meal: Steak and rice.

Favorite musical performers: Matthew Good Band, Third Eye Blind, Ludacris, Elvis.

Favorite actors: Tom Hanks, Vince Vaughn.

Favorite actresses: Susan Ward, Meg Ryan.

Hobbies: Computer games, music, hunting, and "chillin'."

Vehicles: Lots, including a 1971 Corvette, 1999 Corvette, and 1968 Camaro.

If he wasn't racing: "I'd be working at my dad's Chevrolet dealership," he says through his PR representative, Jade Gurss. "It was only a couple of years ago that I was the fastest oil-change man in the place."

"You would never have seen Dale Earnhardt, Sr., in an MTV video," said Gappens with a laugh.[6]

Gappens has been around NASCAR for a long time. He knows the tracks, the fans, the drivers, and who is getting the biggest cheers. Without hesitating, he said it's Dale Earnhardt, Jr.: "He is the buzz."[7]

2

THE TWO BIGGEST RACES

Daytona and Dale Jr.—in the world of NASCAR, and in all of sports—are a magical combination of speed, courage, victory, and cheers.

First on July 7, 2001, and then on February 15, 2004, Dale Jr. took the biggest race in NASCAR on its biggest track, Daytona International Speedway. The first win was full of heartbreak and tears. The second cemented Dale Jr.'s place at the top of the NASCAR heap as he won the race everyone dreams of winning from the first time they slip behind the wheel—the Daytona 500. This one produced tears, too.

After the finish of what turned out to be one of the greatest races in NASCAR history—and possibly one of the greatest sports events of any kind in modern times—Dale Jr. summed it up better than anyone else ever could.

"This," he told reporters waiting to record his every word in their notepads, "is like you can't write a better script."[1]

On the night of July 7, 2001, the son of a legend won the Pepsi 400 at Daytona International Speedway, taking the checkered flag less than five months after his father crashed and died—at the same speedway on the final lap of the famous Daytona 500. It was the first NASCAR Winston Cup race back on the 2.5-mile track where the sport's greatest star had been killed on February 18. It was the first Daytona race since 1979 in which Dale Earnhardt had not competed. Everyone was watching

★ ★ ★ ★ ★ ★ ★ ★ ★ ★ ★ ★ ★ ★ ★ ★

FACT

Dale Earnhardt, Jr., capped a great 2003 season by winning two races and finishing third in the points standings for the entire season. He then picked up where he left off by opening the 2004 season with a win in racing's greatest event—the Daytona 500, where his father lost his life on the last lap in 2001.

to see how his son would handle the pressure, the speed, the competition, and the emotions of racing on the track where he had lost his dad.

Dale Jr.—or Little E as he has become known in racing—was up to the challenge.

Just like his dad had done so many times, he charged from seventh place to first in the final six laps of the 160-lap race to take the 3rd Winston Cup win of his career. But this will always stand as his greatest win, no matter how many more there are to come. And he did it to the cheers of 180,000 who had come hoping for a moment like this, and another 25 million or so more who were watching on TV.

"Man, I just don't know what to say," Dale Jr. was quoted in newspapers as saying after the victory, and after spinning his flaming red No. 8 Chevrolet to celebrate in the infield grass as thousands screamed and cheered. "He [his father] was with me tonight. I don't know how I did it. I dedicate this win to him. I want to say hey to Teresa [Dale Earnhardt's widow] back home. I hope she's loving this, because we are."[2]

The night no race fan will ever forget was capped by fireworks that lit up the Florida sky.

To win a NASCAR race, you need the courage to go 200 miles per hour (mph), and more. You need amazing reflexes to avoid hitting the car just inches

Fans at the Pepsi 400 in Daytona, Florida, hold up three fingers during the third lap of the race as a salute to the late Dale Earnhardt, Sr., on July 7, 2001. Earnhardt lost his life at the 2001 Daytona 500 just five months earlier.

in front of yours. You need a well-built car and a great crew chief and pit crew to keep the engine purring. You need exactly the right strategy so you know when to pass another car, when to hold back, and when to come into the pit for new tires and a tank of gas. When everything is working perfectly on a Saturday night or Sunday afternoon, sometimes you also need a whole lot of good luck to finish first.

The NASCAR drivers run Daytona and a few of the other superspeedways under what they call restrictor-plate rules. Engineers and race officials order that the cars be designed in such a way as to reduce the speeds just enough to make it safer for everyone and to make sure no driver is so fast that he races away from the crowd for an easy win.

Dale Jr. led 116 of the 160 laps. But as at most NASCAR races, leading early does not always mean you are going to lead late. The driver and his crew know how to stay out of trouble, waiting for just the right moment for the driver to put his foot down on the accelerator and make his run for the lead close to the finish.

This race, for all the wrecks and strategy, did not really begin for Dale Jr. until Lap 150—just eleven laps from the checkered flag that flies at the finish line.

A wreck that had damaged ten cars—but not Dale Jr.'s—brought out a caution flag, which means the drivers must slow down quite a bit until officials can get the track cleaned off and ready for high-speed racing. Dale Jr. had been ahead of the wreck, which meant he was able to go to pit road and get four new tires put on his car in a matter of seconds by his crack pit crew. That gave him better traction, which gave him more speed.

The green flag flew on Lap 150, allowing the drivers to put the "pedal to the metal" and roar back to full speed. But it did not last long. On the first lap under green, the Chevrolet Monte Carlo of superstar driver Jeff Gordon began leaking oil and smoking badly. Another caution slowed the drivers once more.

Dale Jr. was looking at six cars in front of him at this late point in the race. He knew the time had come: It was now or never.

Dale Jr. led 116 of the 160 laps. But leading early does not mean you are going to lead late.

With just six laps left, the green flag came out again. Dale Jr. knew what he had to do and how much time he had to do it in. Within one lap he had moved up to third place. On Lap 156, with just four to go, he raced Dave Blaney into second place on the backstretch, then did the same to a determined

Johnny Benson on Turn 4 to take the lead. Turn 4 was not far from the spot where his father was killed.

The Pepsi 400 was far from finished, though, and Dale Jr. knew it. Bobby Labonte, a tough, veteran competitor and the Winston Cup champion from the season before, was right on his bumper waiting for any mistake by Dale Jr. to race around him for the lead. Drivers will tell you there is nothing more frightening than looking into your rearview mirror and seeing another superstar on your back bumper.

But then on Lap 159, one lap from the finish, Labonte was passed by Dale Jr.'s friend and team- mate Michael Waltrip. Waltrip had won the Daytona 500, the race in which Dale Earnhardt was killed. They were part of the same race team. Now in the last seconds of the Pepsi 400, he was right behind Dale Jr., serving as a "blocker," which meant that no other competitor was going to get past the leader and eventual winner.

"Quite frankly, I was thankful," said Waltrip, whose older brother, Darrell, is a NASCAR Winston Cup legend. "At the end of the race, I just pushed him [Dale Jr.]. I am just so thankful that he won, first of all, and that I was able to fight my way through there and run second so I could be part of his celebration."[3]

Dale Earnhardt, Jr., (8) finishes first in the Pepsi 400 in Daytona, Florida, on July 7, 2001. Coming in second is Michael Waltrip and finishing third is Elliott Sadler.

With the crowd roaring in the stands and millions more watching from home on TV, not believing the fairy-tale ending, Dale Jr. climbed through the window of his No. 8 car, as all drivers do, climbed onto the roof, and pumped his fists over and over.

Then up drove teammate Waltrip, who got out of his No. 15 NAPA Chevrolet and climbed onto the roof, where he was joined by Dale Jr. for another big celebration.

The two young athletes did not have to say much to each other. Just a few words were needed.

"I told him, 'This is what it's all about,'" said Waltrip.[4]

The NFL ends its year with its biggest game, the Super Bowl. Major League Baseball caps its season

★ ★ ★ ★ ★ ★ ★ ★ ★ ★ ★ ★ ★ ★

FACT

The owner of Tony Stewart's race team is known for being pretty good in another sport. Washington Redskins coach Joe Gibbs, who has won both the Super Bowl and a NASCAR championship, is also the owner of his own race team featuring Stewart and teammate Bobby Labonte.

with the World Series. NASCAR actually opens its season with the race of all races, the Daytona 500.

When Dale Jr. took the checkered flag on February 15, 2004, it marked the high point of his racing career to that point—and brought tears to everyone's eyes because this was the race in which his dad had died three years before.

On the sixth anniversary, in fact, of the day his dad had won his last Daytona 500, Dale Jr. passed fellow superstar Tony Stewart on Lap 181 and had roared home first. The crowd went wild. Dale Jr. and his good buddy Stewart embraced. Then the winner explained to reporters and the sporting world what winning this one meant.

"All of the things that have happened in the past have made us work harder to try to win this race," Dale Jr. explained. "I'm not ashamed to say I put a lot of emphasis on coming down here and winning this race because of what I have been through down here."[5]

Dale Jr. was a contender from the start, leading the first twenty-nine laps and avoiding a scary twelve-car crash on Lap 71 that took out his friend and teammate Michael Waltrip, whose car flipped three times.

There was the usual give and take, back and

Dale Earnhardt, Jr., hoists the winner's trophy in the victory lane after his dramatic win at the Daytona 500 in 2004.

forth, through the middle of the action—a NASCAR race is more like a marathon than a sprint. But as the laps wound down, it looked like it was going to come down to a duel between Dale Jr. and Stewart.

It happened on Lap 181. Dale Jr. went outside and then back to the inside coming off the fourth turn to begin his pass for the lead. He even picked up a boost from air rushing off Stewart's No. 20 Home Depot car. Stewart tried to pass him back, but Dale Jr. would have none of that.

"When he decided to pull the pin," Stewart said afterward, "he was gone. There wasn't going to be any stopping him."[6]

> "All of the things that have happened in the past have made us work harder to try to win this race."
> —Dale Earnhardt, Jr.

When it was over, Dale Jr. took the traditional victory lap that all winners do, then parked his car at the start-finish line, saluted the cheering fans, and dove into his teammates. He then climbed back into his car and spun his car in the soft Florida grass, the same way his dad had done when he had won the race in 1998.

Dale Jr. won nearly $1.5 million. But winning the Daytona 500 was worth a lot more than money.

"He was over in the passenger seat riding with

me," Dale Jr. said. "I'm sure he was having a blast. . . . I don't know if I will ever be able to tell this story to anybody and really get it right. It's the greatest race. It's the greatest day of my life."[7]

It was an amazing way to start off what would become an incredible season for Dale Earnhardt, Jr.

3

NASCAR ON THE MOVE

Americans still love football, baseball, and basketball. But the love of NASCAR is gaining ground fast. And if some of the young, hot drivers keep on winning races and winning over fans, it might not be long before stock car racing roars past all of our other games to become the nation's number one spectator sport.

"I love the speed," says Johnny Thomas of Sanford, North Carolina, who has followed the sport for twenty-two of his twenty-nine years. "Watching these guys get out there racing, the challenge they have. . . . Of course, everyone loves the wrecks!"[1]

How popular has NASCAR grown since getting

its start in the countryside, small towns, and out-of-the-way dirt tracks of the South after World War II?

Nextel Cup is the biggest and most popular of the eleven divisions in NASCAR, sort of like the major league of the sport. It was called Winston Cup for more than thirty years, named for the famous cigarette produced by R.J. Reynolds Tobacco Company, which paid to be the sponsor. The Nextel Communications company paid $700 million to be the new sponsor for ten years. The sport made the change in part because it did not seem right to have a cigarette maker helping promote the sport to children and families.[2]

NASCAR almost always draws one hundred thousand fans or more to each of its thirty-six Nextel Cup races each season. The Brickyard 400 at the

★ ★ ★ ★ ★ ★ ★ ★ ★ ★ ★ ★ ★ ★ ★

FACT

NASCAR, the major league of stock car racing, stands for the National Association of Stock Car Auto Racing. Since 1980, attendance at races has quadrupled, to 6.7 million fans in 2003. In 2003, 189 million households tuned to a race on TV. It trails only the NFL in attendance.

famous Indianapolis Motor Speedway leads the way with three hundred thousand fans, followed by the Daytona 500 with two hundred thousand. That's bigger than a lot of cities!

In addition to just being in smaller towns like Bristol, Tennessee, and Darlington, South Carolina, NASCAR also draws big crowds to races in the Boston, Chicago, Kansas City, and Miami areas. In 2002, in fact, seventeen of the country's twenty best-attended sports events were Winston Cup races.[3]

Since 1980, attendance at NASCAR races has quadrupled. That means four times more fans—a total of 6.7 million—saw the races in person in 2003.

A poll by *Sports Illustrated* magazine found that 57 percent of fans attend two to four races per year. Forty-eight percent travel 200 miles or more to attend a race, and 25 percent travel an amazing 500 miles or more for the chance to cheer their favorite drivers on to victory.[4]

NASCAR is second only to football in its TV ratings. That means that except for the NFL, more people will watch a race from Daytona or Talladega than any ball game. An average of 7.8 million fans tune in to each race on TV. In all, 189 million total households tuned in to a race on TV in 2003. Added up, the sport claims a total of 75 million loyal fans.

NASCAR estimates that fans spend about $2 billion a year on souvenirs and other items sold in sporting goods stores and at the tracks—caps, jackets, cups, bumper stickers, key chains, anything that can hold the name of Jeff Gordon, Kevin Harvick, Matt Kenseth, or any of the other young, talented drivers taking the sport by storm.

That same *Sports Illustrated* poll found that one out of every five fans said they spent one thousand dollars or more on NASCAR goods in the preceding year, and more than nine out of ten said they bought at least one item the past year. Some of the most fun that fans have at the races is going from one trailer packed with souvenirs to another until they find just the right Dale Earnhardt, Jr., keepsake!

Bill Vincent runs Trademark Sports Cards a mile or so from Lowe's Motor Speedway near Charlotte. He says NASCAR fans are some of his most loyal customers, flocking to his store to buy miniature race cars and trading cards. Where once young sports fans bought baseball cards, now they buy NASCAR cards, with the most popular being Dale Jr. and his father.

What makes NASCAR so hot? Fans and experts will tell you that Americans really love their cars, and really love driving. That means they get a thrill out of watching a driver take an American-made car a lot like theirs and make it go 200 miles per hour around the track. The NASCAR cars—from a Chevrolet Monte Carlo to a Ford Mustang—have always looked a lot like the ones sitting in the family driveway, at least until you pull up the hood and see what the mechanics have done to the engine!

That makes it much easier for people to relate to the sport. NASCAR has done a great job of helping make its drivers accessible to the fans. Just about every one of the drivers will make appearances at public events and autograph signings and stop to talk to fans of all ages. It helps that there always seem to be a bunch of top-notch drivers who are young, handsome, and easy to cheer for—stars like Dale Jr., 2002 champion Tony Stewart, and 2003 champion Matt Kenseth.

The average age of a race winner in 2003, in fact, was thirty-two. That's the lowest it has been since 1968. The top seven drivers in 2003 were all thirty two years of age or younger.

NASCAR fan Thomas is like a lot of other fans. He was introduced to the sport by his dad, Duane, and as he grew up, they watched and cheered together. J. D. McDuffie, a distant cousin, was a

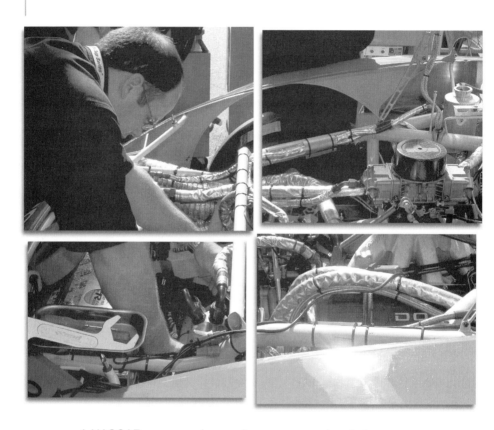

A NASCAR crew member works on a car engine during pre-race preparations before the Siemens 300 in Loudon, New Hampshire, on July 25, 2004.

veteran driver who died in a 1991 wreck at the track in Watkins Glen, New York.

Thomas says the sport has grown for a lot of reasons: the colorful paint schemes of the cars, the enthusiasm of the fans, the friendliness of the drivers, the amazing sight of all those fans packed into a speedway, and the fact that big companies such as Nextel are now helping to bring in new fans through their TV commercials and other promotions.

Like so many others, Thomas was a big fan of Dale Earnhardt. Now he loves Dale Jr. best. "Dad and son," he says. "It just kind of transferred."[5]

NASCAR came roaring out of the hills and dirt tracks of the rural South in the middle of the twentieth century. The story goes that NASCAR's roots trace back to the moonshine days, when the men who made illegal liquor would outrun the law in their souped-up cars. That led to small races on out-of-the-way tracks, which eventually led Bill France, Sr., of Daytona Beach, Florida, to organize a meeting of stock car racing leaders. Out of that meeting in December 1947 came NASCAR, which held its first race on February 15, 1948, at the beach course in Daytona.[6]

The Winston Cup Series started in 1949, and it was off and running from there. Superstar drivers

"The King" Richard Petty flashes a big smile after winning the Daytona 500 for the fourth time in his illustrious career on February 19, 1973.

such as Lee Petty and his son Richard "The King" Petty, were joined by other legends of the sport such as Junior Johnson, Fireball Roberts, David Pearson, and Cale Yarborough. Their colorful names and personalities added to the excitement as big, new tracks were built and TV began showing the races.

To this day no one has more wins than the 200 earned by Richard Petty before he retired. Now Petty is a NASCAR team owner and his son Kyle Petty is a NASCAR driver.

One of the things that Thomas loves most about NASCAR is that the drivers still have to earn their way to the top. From "The King" to Dale Jr., they have not forgotten the simple roots of the sport.

"They still know where they came from," he says. "It wasn't handed to them on a silver platter. In NASCAR, you have to prove you're good."[7]

To get you ready for the races and to become a real fan of Dale Jr., you need to know your NASCAR definitions:

A race begins when an official or guest celebrity says, "Drivers, start your engines!" and an official waves a green flag. A yellow (or caution) flag means there has been a wreck or some other form of trouble, and drivers are to slow down, stay in order, and

FACT

NASCAR stars compete on three types of tracks designed to test their driving ability and give the fans a different experience each weekend. Superspeedways such as Talladega (Alabama) are long, relatively straight, and really fast. Short tracks like Bristol are about a half-mile around and feature a lot of close calls and actual crashes. Short tracks test the drivers' ability to stay out of trouble. Road courses at Watkins Glen in New York and Sears Point in California take drivers through slower, figure-eight style courses meant to test their ability to shift gears and maneuver through tight corners.

wait for the racing to resume. A checkered flag means the race is over.

The drivers are in stock cars, stripped of everything but a driver's seat, doors, and safety equipment. To get a change of tires or a tank of gas or to make changes to their cars during a race, they drive onto pit road so their pit crew can get the job done in a matter of seconds.

Drafting is a common race strategy. It refers to the airflow around a car. A driver will pull up very close to a faster car in front of his in order to take advantage of the reduced air pressure caused by the draft, or airflow, to keep him close to the faster car.

Straightaway is the straight part of the racetrack where drivers can go as fast as possible until they have to slow down in the turns.

★ ★ ★ ★ ★ ★ ★ ★ ★ ★ ★ ★ ★ ★ ★ ★

FACT

The three biggest names in the history of racing? You could start a lively argument with that one during a rain delay at one of the tracks. But you might throw out the names of these three legends to get the talking going: Richard Petty, Dale Earnhardt, Sr., and Junior Johnson.

★ ★ ★ ★ ★ ★ ★ ★ ★ ★ ★ ★ ★ ★

FACT

NASCAR is a walking, talking commercial. Each race car driver's team is sponsored by a number of companies that put up millions of dollars for the right to have their logo and name on the car and on the driver's uniform. Walk into any Home Depot store, for example, and you'll see a giant cardboard cutout of Tony Stewart. And the first thing Tony Stewart says when he wins a race? The Home Depot car ran great today!

When a driver tells his crew chief that his car is "too loose" or "too tight," it means it needs mechanical adjustments so that it can better handle the turns.

At qualifying, drivers must complete one lap in as fast a time as possible. The fastest qualifier starts the race first, the second fastest second, and so on. The driver who starts first has won what is known as the pole position.

Victory Lane, of course, is where the winning driver goes after he has crossed the finish line, taken the checkered flag, and accepted the trophy and the cheers of the crowd.

A.J. Foyt (10) looks as if he is about to run up under Bobby Unser's Camaro (12) while he drafts during a race at the Daytona Speedway in 1975. "Drafting" is the practice of pulling up very close behind another car and using the reduced air pressure to stay close to him.

Now you have a better idea of the great history of the sport in which Dale Earnhardt, Jr., races; how much courage and skill it takes to finish first and be a star; and how many people are cheering him on from the speedways and their living rooms.

And it also helps to have a strong family standing behind you.

4

A FAMILY TRADITION

Country music star Hank Williams, Jr., sings a song that describes his own life. It is all about how he followed in the footsteps of his father, Hank Williams, Sr., a true country music legend who died well before his time.

The classic song is called "Family Tradition," and it could easily have been written in honor of Dale Earnhardt, Jr., and NASCAR. Dale Jr. has not only followed in the footsteps of his legendary father, Dale Sr., but is keeping alive a family tradition that dates all the way back to his grandfather, Ralph.

And just as Hank Williams lost his dad much too soon, so too did Dale Jr.

Like grandfather, like father, and now like son, the Earnhardt name is one of the most famous, not just in NASCAR, but in all of sports. It is just one of many great examples of how sons can often become the sports stars their fathers were before them.

In the NFL, there is Indianapolis Colts quarterback Peyton Manning coming along after his superstar father, Archie, who starred at the University of Mississippi and then the New Orleans Saints. In Major League Baseball, slugger Barry Bonds of the San Francisco Giants followed Bobby Bonds to baseball stardom in San Francisco, just as Ken Griffey, Jr., is a chip off the old block of his father, Ken Griffey, Sr., in Cincinnati. In the NBA, high-scoring forward Rick Barry was followed by his sons, Jon and Brent. In the National Hockey League (NHL), the best example of sons following fathers is Brett Hull taking after his dad, Bobby Hull, "The Golden Jet."

NASCAR has had its share of great family names. You can look to Lee Petty and then his son Richard "The King" Petty, famous for his victories (and sunglasses!), who was followed to the track by his son Kyle. Sadly, Kyle's son Adam was killed in 2000 while practicing at New Hampshire International Speedway. He was just nineteen years old.

The NASCAR family tradition continues today

Dale Earnhardt, Sr., (left) and his son Dale Jr. watch from the pit area at Daytona International Speedway just days before the fateful Daytona 500 race in February 2001.

with Ned Jarrett and his son Dale, a former Winston Cup season champion, a great role model and family man, and a mainstay on today's circuit.

But no name has lit up the tracks for as long as the Earnhardts. It surely has something to do with all three Earnhardts having the courage and talent for driving a race car really fast. But it also has to do with family members passing on their love of the sport and their determination, just as a doctor might get his son excited about medicine or a lawyer might get his daughter interested in the law.

In the small-town South, where the Earnhardts were raised, passing on their passion is what family members have done proudly from generation to generation.

"That's what blue-collar people do," H. A. "Humpy" Wheeler of Lowe's Motor Speedway outside Charlotte told the *Washington Post*'s Liz Clarke several years ago. "They teach their kids to weld if they're a welder or plumb if they're a plumber. Some of them make it, and some of them don't."[1]

The Earnhardts definitely made it—one after another after another!

It all started in small-town Kannapolis, North Carolina, with Ralph Earnhardt. Dale Jr.'s grandfather was considered a pioneer of the sport. In fact, he

★ ★ ★ ★ ★ ★ ★ ★ ★ ★ ★ ★ ★ ★ ★

FACT

Dale Earnhardt, Sr., won 76 races and 7 series championships on the Winston Cup circuit before he died at the Daytona 500 in 2001. He was nicknamed "The Intimidator" for his aggressive driving style and because he hid his emotions behind his trademark sunglasses.

was named one of NASCAR's fifty best drivers of all time. But he started small, working on race cars in his shop, building cars for other people, and racing on the many short dirt tracks that dotted the South fifty or so years ago.

Longtime NASCAR writer Bob Myers remembers watching Ralph Earnhardt wreck a car in Atlanta early in his career, a mishap he was determined to learn from.

Ralph Earnhardt was not much of a talker; he did not promote himself the way some athletes do today. He just concentrated on the sport he loved, and he was as good as anyone. In his career, which spanned the 1960s and early 1970s, he won more than 500 races, even if he never made much money at it. He did not care, though. Unlike many of today's athletes, who hold out for bigger contracts and do TV commercials to make even more money, he competed for the love of the sport.

Myers said Ralph Earnhardt was a simple man who never wanted to travel or win a lot of fame; he just wanted to work on cars and race them, and pass along his love to his son Dale.

Young Dale responded. He would work in the family shop and then watch his dad race, and often win, on weekends. He remembers fondly counting the seconds in school until he could run home, pick up a tool in his dad's shop, and start fiddling with a race car.

"I'd sit on the back of a flatbed truck, watching him go around and around, and every lap he made, I made," Dale told the *Washington Post* in 1987, at the height of his success. "When I finally sat in a race car, it was like I already knew how to drive."[2]

Myers remembers father and son spending time together at a little half-mile dirt track near the fairgrounds in Charlotte called Metrolina Speedway. "Dale and Ralph would sit on the back of the pickup truck, and Dale would dream of where he was going," Myers said. "He made it!"[3]

Sadly, though, the relationship ended too soon.

Dale Earnhardt, Jr., (8) passes his father, Dale Sr. (3), to take the early lead in the Coca-Cola 600 race at Lowe's Motor Speedway in Concord, North Carolina, on May 28, 2000.

Ralph Earnhardt died of a heart attack in 1973 at age forty-four. It seems fitting that he was working on a car at the time. He left behind a great career, a loyal family, and a son not knowing exactly what to do next.

"Dale Earnhardt, Sr., idolized Ralph," Myers said. "He was devastated when his father died."[4]

Dale told the *Atlanta Journal-Constitution* newspaper, "It was the biggest shock of my life. I didn't know which way to turn, what to do, where to go for help and advice. I was helpless."[5]

It was not long, though, before the heartbroken son found the right way to turn. Having already dropped out of high school, he started earning a living in a gas station, pumping gas and cleaning windshields. By 1971 he was behind the wheel of a car, racing on the dirt tracks around his house, showing a bit of the Earnhardt drive that would take him quickly to the top.

With the help of then–race car driver Harry Gant, who sold Dale a car that could go on asphalt, Dale began racing in the smaller Sportsman division.

In 1975, two years after his dad died, he made his debut in the Winston Cup, the biggest circuit of all, at Charlotte Motor Speedway. He never looked back, racing to the front in his hard-charging style that quickly made him feared by competitors and loved by fans. The seventy-six races he won on the Winston Cup circuit show what a superstar he was before tragedy struck on the last lap at Daytona in 2001.

With his slow Southern drawl and thick mustache Dale looked and sounded the part of the NASCAR star. With his guts and aggressiveness he played the role perfectly, always seeming to push his car like no other driver, always challenging his competitors, even if it meant making them mad.

He had guts, too! Once, as a rookie in 1979, he wrecked and wound up with a concussion and other injuries. He was unconscious when they put him on a stretcher and into a helicopter for the ride to the hospital. He risked injury and the anger of other drivers to always race to the front.

Dale once told the *Washington Post*: "I've seen guys trying to spin my dad out and they'd wreck [themselves]. And I've seen guys trying to spin me and they don't, either, and they run second. If I wanted to wreck someone, I could tell you what hole in the fence I was going to put 'em in. I'm a serious racer and I try to stay within the bounds. I don't do anything unjust. If beating 'em's unjust, they're just going to have to get beat."[6]

Dale Earnhardt, Sr., (left) assists his son, Kerry, as he climbs out of his car after winning the ARCA Pocono 500 race in Long Pond, Pennsylvania, on June 17, 2000. The race was the first victory of Kerry Earnhardt's career.

All the while he was racing and building a winning team, Dale was grooming his three older children to get involved in the sport (his son, Kerry, also became a NASCAR driver, in addition to Dale Jr.). And he did it the right way, just as any good father in any profession would—not handing his kids everything, but making sure they learned from the bottom up as part of the family operation.

It was the way his father had taught him.

"He was very keen on those kids working on those race cars," Wheeler of Lowe's Motor Speedway said. "He wanted them in the shop, and he wanted to see them dirty. And he didn't pay them a lot of money."[7]

It did not take long for one very special Earnhardt child to learn his tough lessons well enough to carry on the family tradition in superstar fashion.

5

FROM THE BEGINNING

From sweeping floors to superstardom—that is the best way to describe the incredible journey that has taken Dale Earnhardt, Jr., to the front of the NASCAR pack. Millions of fans see him today in the flaming red Budweiser No. 8 car and think that with his name and family tradition, he was born to win races and accept the cheers of the crowd. But like his father before him, Dale Jr. was forced to learn the sport from the bottom up. He was given no special treatment. Nobody showed him any shortcuts.

It is not much different from the way anyone learns something that has been in his or her family for years. You start at the bottom. You work hard to work your way up. You look, listen, and soak it all in. And then when your time comes, you're ready to succeed!

From the moment he was born on October 10, 1974, in Concord, North Carolina, to Dale and Brenda Earnhardt, it did not take a genius to see where Dale Earnhardt, Jr., was headed.

Just as Dale Earnhardt grew up working in the race shop of his father, Ralph, Dale Jr. can remember hanging out at his dad's shop and family farm in the rolling countryside north of Charlotte. He would sweep the floors, clean the stables, and follow his dad around, all the while wishing for the day when he, too, could get behind the wheel of some sort of racing machine. Before he learned how to maneuver a car at 200 miles per hour past a dozen other racers, though, he learned about what goes under the hood and what goes on in the race shop. He learned the

★ ★ ★ ★ ★ ★ ★ ★ ★ ★ ★ ★ ★

FACT

Dale Earnhardt, Jr., began his driving career at age seventeen, competing in the street stock division at Concord Motor Speedway near Charlotte, North Carolina.

fundamentals, which you need to know first no matter what you do in life.

He started with go-karts at age thirteen, going as fast as he could with his sister, Kelley—though it was not fast enough to beat their dad through the fields on his four-wheeler.

But Dale Jr. remembers that his dad was not crazy about those go-karts. In a 1998 interview with veteran sportswriter Bob Myers of *Circle Track* magazine, he said his dad did not like the fact that those go-karts lacked seat belts and roll bars. "And I came flying out of them quite often," Dale Jr. recalled.[1]

Like any parent, even daredevil NASCAR superstar Dale Earnhardt feared for his children's safety.

A few years later, Dale Jr. realized what he called a childhood fantasy—he graduated to a race car in the Street Stock division at nearby Concord Motor Speedway. He finished fourth in the first race in which he was legally old enough to compete, at the amazingly young age of seventeen!

Most kids are barely old enough then to drive on the street in front of their home, much less on a racetrack.

Dale Jr. played a little soccer growing up. He went to several schools before finally graduating from Mooresville (North Carolina) High School,

Dale Earnhardt, Jr., (8) is about to pass Jeff Gordon during the final laps of the NASCAR Checker Auto Parts 500 race in November 2004. Dale's grandfather, Ralph Earnhardt, also raced under the number eight.

admitting that he was not cut out to be a bookworm or a brain. He knew early on that he was cut out to race cars.

"I saw firsthand how competitive and enjoyable racing was, and what it was all about," Dale Jr. told Myers.[2]

NASCAR is a lot like baseball, in that you move up from the minor leagues to the major leagues. This is what Dale Jr. did, going from go-karts to street stocks to the late model division of the Winston Racing Series. These are less powerful cars that do not go as fast as the ones the fans see on Sunday. From 1994 to 1996, Dale Jr. had 90 Top 10 finishes in 113 races, winning three of them.

Better than that, he learned that it took steadiness to survive and succeed on the racetrack.

"In the Winston racing, I helped put together, work on and set up my cars," he told Bob Myers, one of the most experienced sportswriters, who has covered NASCAR for years. "I learned from my mistakes and that's paying off now. I wasn't a dominating driver, didn't win many races, but I was consistent."[3]

Next up for Dale Jr. came the Busch Grand National Series—comparable to the highest level of the minor leagues in baseball before you make it to Yankee Stadium in the major leagues. These racers

Dale Earnhardt, Jr., began racing go-karts like the ones above when he was just thirteen years old.

usually compete on Saturday afternoons at the same track where the NASCAR drivers race on Sundays; some of the NASCAR Sunday boys even go at it against the Busch Series drivers on Saturdays. The Busch guys love to go up against the big names.

But not even the biggest stars of the sport could keep up with Dale Jr. in his No. 3 ACDelco Chevrolet. In 1998 and 1999 he took home the Busch Grand National Series title, becoming the first driver to win such a championship after both his father and grandfather had won it before him. During those two magical years Dale Jr. won 13 races and more than $3 million in prize money. Along with other young guns Matt Kenseth, Casey Atwood, and Adam Petty (from the famed Lee and Richard Petty racing family), Dale Jr. became part of the so-called Brat Pack of racing.

Each Saturday, with crowds starting to buzz about the next Earnhardt superstar in the sport, Dale Jr. began showing the hard-charging style that made his family famous.

"Aggressive, more so at times than it should be, relative to the way NASCAR runs the series" he told Myers when asked to describe how he drives. "I enjoy that kind of racing, hate watching a race that looks like a bunch of toy soldiers marching around.

Fans like action, even if their favorite driver gets bumped around or spun out."[4]

Fans really liked the action that Dale Jr. gave them. And it did not take an expert to see that a true turning point for Dale Jr. came in Fort Worth, Texas, on April 4, 1998. It was the Coca-Cola 300 at the beautiful new Texas Motor Speedway, and Dale Jr. was making his sixteenth start in the Busch Grand National Series, in the car his dad owned. He had not won a race yet, but that had not kept the eyes of the sport from turning to the young man many hoped might become a superstar.

Starting in the middle of the pack, Dale Jr. had held his own throughout the race, staying out of trouble, making his pit stops, and putting himself in

★ ★ ★ ★ ★ ★ ★ ★ ★ ★ ★ ★ ★ ★ ★ ★

FACT

"The Young Guns" is a nickname that has been given to the popular young stars of Nextel Cup, led by Dale Earnhardt, Jr., Kevin Harvick, Matt Kenseth, Tony Stewart, Jeff Gordon, and Jimmie Johnson. If you do not catch them racing on the track, you can catch them endorsing various products in many TV commercials.

a position to challenge for the lead when the right time came.

That time came with just eleven laps to go.

Starting third on a restart after a mishap involving another driver brought out a caution flag to slow down the field, Dale Jr. found himself trailing Glenn Allen and Joe Nemechek. But Allen spun into the infield following another mishap, and now there was only Nemechek standing between Dale Jr. and the checkered flag.

With six laps to go, Earnhardt avoided being hit by Stanton Barrett, whose car spun into the wall in Turn 2. Then on the final lap, Earnhardt got under Nemechek coming out of Turn 4, which means he drove to the inside of his rival and got to Turn 1 with the lead. Nemechek was on older tires, which means they were not gripping the track as well and his car could not keep up.

Roaring at more than 176 miles per hour—the fastest by any race leader during the day—Dale Jr. held off Nemechek and a hard-charging Elliott Sadler and crossed the finish line first.

He had roared to the lead on the last lap to win!

The crowd cheered, and all the Earnhardts celebrated, with father and son sharing hugs in Victory Lane.

"That was pretty awesome, wasn't it?" Dale Earnhardt, Sr., told sports reporters after he had helped coach his son through the race via their two-way radio. "I couldn't be prouder. That felt as good as it did when I won the Daytona 500."[5]

Afterward, Dale Jr. called the embrace with his father one of the most emotional moments of his life. "It stirred memories of the years I had tried so hard to earn my dad's approval," he told Bob Myers of *Circle Track* magazine. "Maybe that did it. It really was a proud moment for him to show that much excitement and happiness over something that I had accomplished."[6]

Earlier, Dale Jr. had said something else to reporters, that after his dad's death, really hits home today: "I win to put smiles on his face," Dale Jr. said. "I don't care much about anything else as far as the bonuses that come along with winning—the money, the exposure, the fame—it's all just to make him happy. That's what it's all about to me."

Then he said something that brings a tear to the eye, knowing what we know now: "He's my daddy and I love him to death and I want to do it for him."[7]

Life has not been easy for Dale Jr. It hardly ever is for anyone who has big dreams and sets out to make them come true.

Pole sitter Elliott Sadler (66) and Joe Nemecheck (87) lead the pack at the beginning of the Coca-Cola 300 at the Texas Motor Speedway on April 4, 1998. Dale Earnhardt, Jr., would go on to take the race for the first victory of his pro career.

He had to grow up in the shadow of his famous father and of his grandfather Ralph—the racing legend he never knew. Dale Jr. had to race cars knowing the fans would always compare him to those two other racing Earnhardts. That was a lot of pressure to have to deal with.

Like so many kids today, he was the child of divorce, living first with his mother, Brenda, and then with his father and his new wife, Teresa. Today, Teresa Earnhardt is involved in the Earnhardt racing empire her late husband built, and is very close to Dale Jr. Their great relationship is a wonderful example of how families can come together after a divorce.

And, of course, years later his father's death at Daytona changed everything.

Through it all, the tall, lanky, talented youngster with racing in his blood kept his eyes on the goal he had set out for himself years before.

That goal was about to carry him to American racing's greatest stage.

6

PHENOM!

T he clever people who are part of NASCAR never miss a trick when it comes to promoting their events and finding that one neat angle to a race that will really get the fans revved up to cheer.

One of the greatest moments in recent NASCAR history came on May 30, 1999, at Lowe's Motor Speedway. It was Memorial Day weekend, probably the most popular weekend of the year for race fans across America. The eyes of all fans were turned to the giant track outside Charlotte.

There, competing in his first Winston Cup race, was Dale Earnhardt, Jr. Starting eighth out of forty-three cars in his No. 8 Chevrolet, the son of living legend Dale Earnhardt was finally going to take the green flag in stock car racing's highest league. Finally, Little E was taking his place beside his dad and all the other superstar drivers who push their machines to the limit.

His No. 8 was a perfect fit—it was the number of his grandfather Ralph's car way back when and the number his father, Dale, used in the early stages of his career, before switching to his famous No. 3.

No wonder, given all this, that Dale Jr.'s sponsor gave his Winston Cup debut its very own title—Countdown to E-Day! There was pressure on the young driver, but it was the kind of pressure he had waited a lifetime to face.

"When that motor cranks," Dale Jr. told the *Charlotte Observer*, "it drowns out all of the other thoughts and everything that's going on. You roll out on the racetrack and just forget about it. That's the quickest way to remedy all of the pressure."[1]

In practice the day before his debut, Dale Jr. had raced his car all the way up to 176.321 mph—second fastest among the drivers. Still, given his lack of experience and all the fanfare surrounding the race, the young driver was not going to get too cocky. He said:

> Realistically, anything can happen to us here. It's our first Winston Cup race. We've got a lot

Dale Earnhardt, Jr., signs autographs for fans at Michigan Speedway in Brooklyn, Michigan, on August 18, 2000.

to overcome, a lot of situations that have been thrown in our face. . . . But that's good. We need to go ahead and face the music here, to get down to business and get good at it as quick as we can.[2]

In front of nearly two hundred thousand race fans, most of them cheering themselves hoarse for him, Dale Jr. did not win the first time out with the big guns. But he surely did not disappoint.

He finished 16th—ten spots behind his father— as Jeff Burton outdueled Bobby Labonte to win it all. After the race Dale Jr. told reporters his car was "loose"—NASCAR talk for not being able to maneuver crisply enough in the turns. But by the way he said it, you could tell that the thrill of racing was more powerful than the disappointment of not winning. "It was a lot of fun," Dale Jr. told reporters. "I hope those drivers out there are a little bit more comfortable with me. I was just trying not to tear up a race car and earn some respect, and to learn something from running around with them out there."[3]

That exciting debut in 1999 was just the start of a career that really took off in 2000—Dale Jr.'s first full year on the Winston Cup circuit. Now he was going to go up against the big boys each and every weekend.

It was not easy, of course—nothing worth

achieving in sports or in life ever is. Over three straight weekends of racing, he finished 29th in Atlanta with car problems after slamming into the wall, then crashed at both Darlington, South Carolina, and Bristol, Tennessee, and did not finish at all.

No one around NASCAR doubted that Dale Jr. was going to eventually make his way to the front of the pack. They just wondered when it might happen. Well, they did not have to wait long. On April 2, 2000, in front of a sellout crowd of 223,000 at the amazing, new Texas Motor Speedway in Fort Worth, Texas, Dale Jr. started out from the fourth position and roared to the front of the DIRECTV 500 to take the checkered flag. He beat runner-up Jeff Burton by nearly six seconds—a huge margin in a NASCAR race.

In just his twelfth start in the Winston Cup, Dale Jr. had taken the win—even better than his dad, who needed sixteen races to get that first big one.

And no wonder Texas will always have a soft spot in Dale Jr.'s heart—Texas Motor Speedway is also where he won his first race in the Busch Series.

"I'm kind of overwhelmed by what's happened here," Dale Jr. told reporters crowded around him to get the big story of his first NASCAR win.[4]

Dale Sr. finished 7th at Texas, but it did not douse

Jeff Gordon (left) shares a laugh with Dale Earnhardt, Jr.

his excitement by a long shot—his son had won his first one!

"It took a lot of hard work, and I knew it would just be a matter of time before [Dale Jr.] won," the proud father told the press. "He talked about winning his first race at Texas."[5]

Dale Jr. dominated the race, but that does not mean there were not some close calls. When you get forty cars going 200 mph or so around the track, trouble is never far away. The race averaged a wreck every thirty seconds, which means Dale Jr. was dodging the competition and taking on four tires at every pit stop to make sure his car could grip the track. After he pulled away from Bobby Labonte and Burton, Dale Jr. crossed the finish line with everyone else way back in his rearview mirror.

Following the win members from several other teams rushed to congratulate Dale Jr.—they knew this was history in the making. But everyone also knew who the true celebration would center around.

When Dale Sr. got to his son, the two embraced.

"He just said he loved me, and he wanted to make sure I enjoyed today," Dale Jr. said.

The rookie season turned out to be a big one for Dale Jr. He won the Pontiac Excitement 400 in Richmond; became the first rookie to win the popular

★ ★ ★ ★ ★ ★ ★ ★ ★ ★ ★ ★ ★ ★ ★

FACT

Dale Earnhardt, Jr., is among the most popular drivers in NASCAR, and one of the most popular athletes in any sport. He was chosen for People magazine's "50 Most Eligible Bachelors" special edition in 2002, and has appeared in music videos with Sheryl Crow and 3 Doors Down.

all-star race at Lowe's Motor Speedway, The Winston; and finished 16th for the year in the points totals. The season champion is the one who accumulates the most points by finishing consistently near the front over the course of the long season.

Dale Jr. was headed into the 2001 season, not just as the son of a legend, but as a great driver in his own right. He was already being tabbed to be a superstar, one who could rise up and challenge superstar Jeff Gordon for king of the hill. The two were young, handsome, bright, and full of energy. What a rivalry people thought this could be.

"If we turn into steady rivals," Dale Jr. was quoted as saying in the *Dallas Morning News*, "it is just going to produce more race fans—more race fans for him and more race fans for me. If I can be that competitive, I'll be really happy."[6]

The 2001 season, then, was supposed to be the one that propelled Dale Jr. to the front of the track and the front of the sports pages.

Tragedy changed all that.

7

TRAGEDY ON THE LAST LAP

It happened late in the afternoon of February 18, 2001, on the last lap of the Daytona 500, the most famous NASCAR race of them all.

NASCAR would never be the same. Neither would the Earnhardt family, the first family of racing. Neither would the young man who cried over the death of his dad—but who kept the promise he made to himself and his fans: that the loss would inspire him to race that much harder.

When you are Dale Earnhardt, Jr.—when you carry the most famous name in the sport—racing hard is what you do.

The day of the Daytona 500 dawned like any

other race day for Dale Earnhardt, Sr., even if this was the first race of the year and the one every driver wanted to win the most.

The Man in Black, The Intimidator as he was known, attended the drivers' meeting at around 11:00 A.M. with his wife, Teresa. The meeting ended with a chaplain asking the Lord for a safe race.

Dale Earnhardt, forty-nine, was set to start seventh in the race in his famous black No. 3 Chevrolet. Thirty minutes before the 1:00 P.M. start, he joked with fellow driver Jeff Burton about whether Burton was going to buy a boat, a purchase he was having to talk his wife into.

Just after 1:00 P.M., after receiving the traditional instruction, "Drivers, start your engines," the drivers took off in the Daytona 500. No one could have imagined at the start how this would end.

As in every NASCAR race, the drivers jockeyed for position through the middle portions of the race, looking to stay near the lead but trying to avoid a wreck that could end the day early.

On the fortieth of the two hundred laps, Dale Earnhardt was running a solid 9th. He led on Laps 83 and 84 and settled into a Top 10 position, counting on being there to challenge near the finish. On Lap 174—just twenty-six to go now—a nineteen-car wreck sent young superstar Tony Stewart to the hospital with a concussion and forced the race to stop while the track was cleared of car parts and debris.

When the race resumed to the wild cheers of the fans, there were just twenty-one laps left, maybe thirty minutes until someone was going to wind up whooping and hollering for joy in Victory Lane.

Lap 180 found Dale Earnhardt, Jr., leading the 500-mile race, with Dale Sr. trailing close behind. Then Michael Waltrip, one of their teammates in their racing operation, roared to the lead, followed by Dale Jr., and then Dale Sr. Waltrip was trying to win his first race in 463 tries. And Dale Jr. was about to make good on the prediction that 2001 was going to be the year he shot to superstardom.

The millions watching on TV at home heard Darrell Waltrip, a once-popular driver who now broadcasts the races on TV, screaming from the booth for his younger brother to hold on.

With just a lap to go now, Dale Earnhardt, Sr., Sterling Marlin, and Ken Schrader raced for third place down the backstretch. As they headed through Turn 3, The Man in Black suddenly headed to the lower part of the track, thinking that was the best place to make his final move.

Dale Earnhardt, Sr., (3) runs right behind his son, Dale Jr. (8), near the end of the 2001 Daytona 500, just a few laps prior to his fatal accident.

But suddenly, after grazing another car on his left, he shot to the right, with the front of his No. 3 Chevy pointing toward the concrete wall. That is when it all happened. Schrader's Pontiac, through no fault of the driver, plowed into the right side of Dale Earnhardt's car and sent it head-on into the outside wall at Turn 4.

Waltrip beat his teammate, Dale Jr., across the finish line to take the win. But by that point, many eyes were turned to Dale Sr.'s car, and The Man in Black inside.

Not knowing what the next few moments were about to bring, Darrell Waltrip screamed to the world watching his brother's win on TV: "This is great. I just hope Dale's OK. I guess he's all right, isn't he?"[1]

It did not take long for everyone at Daytona, and everyone around the world watching the race on TV and listening to it on radio, to realize he was not going to be all right.

Ken Schrader jumped from his car to check on Earnhardt, furiously motioning for emergency workers to come help. Dr. Steve Bohannon, the track's director of emergency services, was one of the first to get there, and he knew it was not good within seconds.

"When I walked up and saw what car it was and

then looked in, and the other physician, who was in the car working on him, looked up at me, I could tell," Bohannon told reporters. "It broke my heart."[2]

A few moments later at Halifax Medical Center, not far from the track, The Man in Black was pronounced dead. His wife, Teresa, was at his side.

At around 7:00 P.M., back at Daytona Speedway, NASCAR head Mike Helton had to make it official, telling reporters with a sad voice: "This is undoubtedly one of the most difficult announcements I have personally ever had to make. We've lost Dale Earnhardt."[3]

Forty minutes later, the large American flag at the speedway was slowly lowered to half-staff. Other flags around the country were soon to follow.

In the heartbreaking days to come, race fans would cry over the loss of their hero. But even those who did not know anything about NASCAR understood that a great legend had been lost.

On the day of Earnhardt's memorial service at giant Calvary Church in Charlotte, North Carolina, thousands gathered in restaurants, auditoriums, even outside speedways everywhere to pay their respects and watch the service on national TV. It was a cold, rainy Thursday in the Carolinas, fitting for the sadness that hung like a cloud over the region.

This tribute to Dale Earnhardt, Sr., was displayed at the General Motors world headquarters at the Renaissance Center in Detroit in February 2001.

The Marklein family was typical. They canceled plans to fly home to Wisconsin after a vacation in Las Vegas, and instead flew to Charlotte just so they could be in the heart of NASCAR country for this occasion. They watched the memorial service on three giant TV screens at Founders Hall in uptown Charlotte. Among the hundreds in attendance, they brushed back tears as the prayers and hymns proceeded.

"We came for Dale," Marcy Marklein told the *Charlotte Observer*.

They came, the *Charlotte Observer*'s Scott Fowler wrote, because they loved a driver who always remained close to his roots. "He was the high school dropout from Kannapolis who made good," Fowler wrote. "Then he made great. Then he became a national legend, but he was still ours. Up to and including the day of his death, Earnhardt drove the way other drivers did only in their dreams. He was cunning and utterly fearless. It was as if the No. 3 car winked at the fans each time it sped around the track, saying, 'OK, watch this. You're not going to believe this.'"[4]

And what of Dale Earnhardt, Jr.—the son of the legend, the talented young driver who now would be

★ ★ ★ ★ ★ ★ ★ ★ ★ ★ ★ ★ ★ ★

After his father's death on the last lap of the 2001 Daytona 500, Dale Earnhardt, Jr., reminded people of what is most important in life. He went on The 700 Club TV show and told people, "It [losing a father] shows you how conceited you are, how trifling you can be, how selfish you are. It's really changed me 100 percent, hopefully into a better person."

faced with the awesome challenge of carrying on his beloved father's name in this most dangerous sport?

He gathered with his family after their loss at Daytona to cry together, to attend the memorial service, to draw strength from being with loved ones.

Then he went racing the next weekend in the Dura-Lube 400 at Rockingham, North Carolina.

Going racing, as we know now, is what Dale Earnhardt, Jr., does.

8

SUPERSTAR ON THE RISE

In the days after Dale Earnhardt's death at the Daytona 500, Dale Jr. spoke of the terrible crash making him more religious and helping him to see what's truly important in life. It is not money and fame, he said. It is family and faith and using your talents to the best of your ability.

"It [losing his father] shows you how conceited you are, how trifling you can be, how selfish you are," Dale Jr. told *The 700 Club* TV show in one of his first interviews after Dale Sr.'s death. "It's really changed me a hundred percent, hopefully into a better person."[1]

So off the track, Dale Jr. began growing up after

the tragedy. Always known as a young guy who enjoyed having fun and partying with his friends, he began to become more mature about his life and more serious about his racing. He talked of learning to appreciate his family, his fans, and his sport more.

On the track he kept racing to the top, with no end in sight.

First, he won the Pepsi 400, the first race back at Daytona after his dad's death. He finished third for the entire 2003 season, won two races at Talladega, Alabama, and Phoenix, Arizona, and took home nearly $5 million in prize money. He captured his first Daytona 500 to open the 2004 Nextel Cup season—the Super Bowl of the sport.

He is now considered a contender each year for

★ ★ ★ ★ ★ ★ ★ ★ ★ ★ ★ ★ ★ ★ ★ ★

FACT

Dale Earnhardt, Jr., tries to give back to the community and his fans. In 2003 he donated $5,000 to build a climbing wall at South Elementary School in his hometown of Mooresville so kids can get some exercise instead of just watching TV and playing video games. He even autographed the wall!

the championship that goes to the driver who gains the most points over the course of the season. And in nearly every fan survey taken these days, Dale Jr. wins "most popular driver"—the driver that the fans cheer the most and that companies want to endorse their products and put on the cover of their magazines.

Fame is even sending the Earnhardts into the movies. An ESPN TV movie on the late Dale Earnhardt and his family is titled 3, in honor of his famous black Chevy. The amazing movie *NASCAR: The IMAX Experience* is full of footage of the two Dales and the Earnhardt racing empire. Those who get a 3-D look at NASCAR in their local OMNIMAX theater come away amazed by the speed of the sport, awed by the devotion of the fans, and impressed by Dale Jr. saying he aims for total dominance.[2]

So what is next for the racing superstar? Dale Jr. says he wants to become more of a thinking-man's driver—not just pushing the gas pedal as hard as he can, but knowing when to hold back. He wants to gain the experience to know when to pick his spots on each racetrack, and to learn how to be the respected leader of a team that includes his pit crew, crew chief, engine builders, and all the unsung

Dale Earnhardt, Jr., looks back at the track after completing his qualifying run for the 2004 EA Sports 500 race at Talladega Superspeedway in Talladega, Alabama.

mechanics and office workers back at the race shop in North Carolina.

He wants to be admired, not just for his courage and daring, but for his safety and smarts.

And he says he wants to race until he's forty or forty-five, which means we could be cheering Dale Jr. on until around 2020, so long as he stays safe!

"I do it because it is fun," Dale Jr. said before the start of the 2004 season. "It won't be any fun if I have to do it for somebody else's reasons other than mine. I want to be able to drive and make my own decisions. I don't feel a lot of pressure to be an important figure in the sport. I just want to do it how I want to because I am my own person."[3]

As the twenty-first century unfolds, NASCAR is on the verge of becoming the hottest sport in a nation that loves high speed, huge crowds, daring athletes, and the roar of those engines.

And clearly, these days Dale Jr. has become The Man. Race fans cannot seem to get enough of his simple, direct style—he does not put on any of the fancy airs some other athletes do. What you see is what you get. Whether racing for the win or signing autographs with a smile afterward, he is just Dale Jr. from the North Carolina country, a guy who loves what he is doing and does not mind showing it.

★ ★ ★ ★ ★ ★ ★ ★ ★ ★ ★ ★ ★

FACT

Once asked by a group of North Carolina children whether it is scary to drive a race car, Dale Earnhardt, Jr., said, "When you get in the car, you're nervous, you're very nervous. Kind of like you're going to the first day of school. Every Sunday."

On a nationally televised interview one evening, CNN's Larry King was getting the lowdown on NASCAR from Dale Jr. and that other superstar Jeff Gordon, who is considered Dale Jr.'s biggest rival on the track.

In the middle of the conversation, right about the time Dale Jr. showed off his huge, gleaming Daytona 500 trophy, Jeff Gordon began laughing.

"What's so funny?" King asked Gordon on the air, in front of millions of Americans.

That's when Gordon gave the simple answer that all of the racing world would have given if they were in his shoes. It is the answer that best sums up Dale Earnhardt, Jr., the driver with the famous name who has shot to the top of the sports world and aims to stay there.

"Junior just cracks me up," Gordon said. "We all wish we could be as cool as him!"[4]

The thirteenth NASCAR win for Dale Earnhardt, Jr., was one of his biggest. On August 28, 2004, before some 160,000 screaming fans at Bristol Motor Speedway in Bristol, Tennessee, he took the Sharpie 500 on the famed short track known for its tight racing and spectacular wrecks.

This Nextel Cup win came five years to the day after his dad won at Bristol by bumping Terry Labonte on the final lap. But even more than that, the win was the first for Earnhardt Jr. since he nearly lost his life in a fiery wreck July 18 in Sonoma, California, while racing in the American LeMans Series.

Earnhardt Jr. suffered burns in that wreck, which was replayed over and over on TV stations across the country. As they watched his narrow escape many fans wondered whether he could come back from the burns, and from the fear he said he felt that day in California. The win at Bristol proved he could. As he told reporters: "This is huge for me, it's awesome for our team. We really needed that. My dad made this place magical for Earnhardt fans, and I was one of them. He was The Man. Wherever he's at, he's laughing."[5]

Dale Earnhardt, Jr., waves to the crowd from his car after winning the Sharpie 500 at Bristol Motor Speedway in Bristol, Tennessee, on August 28, 2004.

★ ★ ★ ★ ★ ★ ★ ★ ★ ★ ★ ★ ★ ★

FACT

Want to get up close and personal with NASCAR? Check out NASCAR: The IMAX Experience at an OMNIMAX theater near you and get a 3-D look at the speed, danger and thrills of the sport. You'll feel like you're in the stands at Daytona or riding along with Dale Earnhardt, Jr. at Bristol Motor Speedway in Bristol, Tennessee, one of the sport's most exciting tracks. The coolest quote in the movie? Legend Richard "The King" Petty says he knows exactly when auto racing got started.

"When they built the second car," he says.

The win did even more than prove the young superstar's courage. It helped propel him into the Top 10 in the race for the Nextel Cup championship for 2004, and helped cement his status as NASCAR's most talked-about driver.

Dale Earnhardt Jr.'s race for the championship in the 2004 season would end just short of the top. NASCAR's most popular driver made the Top 10 that competed for the season-ending Nextel Cup championship, but he wound up in fifth place after closing the season with a 23rd place finish at Homestead-Miami Speedway in Homestead, Florida.

Though he trailed champion Kurt Busch by 138 points, he still took home $1.3 million, with pride.

"We had good days, and we had bad days," he said afterward, "but we battled and put together our best season ever."[6]

CHAPTER NOTES

Chapter I. Dale

1. *Sports Illustrated* magazine, special edition devoted to NASCAR, October 27, 2003, p. 24.
2. Ibid.
3. Author interview with Jerry Gappens of Lowe's Motor Speedway, Charlotte, North Carolina, 2004.
4. Ibid.
5. Ibid.
6. Ibid.
7. Ibid.

Chapter 2. The Two Biggest Races

1. David Poole, "Junior's Win Was Storybook Moment," *The Charlotte Observer*, July 9, 2001, p. C1.
2. David Poole, "Earnhardt Conquers Daytona," *The Charlotte Observer*, July 8, 2001, p. C1.
3. Ibid.
4. Ibid.
5. David Poole, "1 for the Son," *The Charlotte Observer*, February 16, 2004, p. C6.
6. Ibid.
7. David Poole, "Junior Gets Win at Track Where He Lost So Much," *The Charlotte Observer*, February 16, 2004, p. C1.

Chapter 3. NASCAR on the Move

1. *Sports Illustrated* magazine, special edition devoted to NASCAR, October 27, 2003, p. 8.
2. "Winston's Sponsorship Stood Test of Time," *Official NASCAR Web Site*, November 17, 2003, <http://www.nascar.com> (November 24, 2003).
3. *Sports Illustrated* magazine, special edition devoted to NASCAR, October 27, 2003, p. 10.
4. Ibid.
5. Ibid.
6. "NASCAR Comes to the Really Big Screen," *Official NASCAR Web Site*, n.d., <http://www.nascar.com> (March 11, 2004).
7. *Sports Illustrated* magazine, special edition devoted to NASCAR, October 27, 2003, p. 11.

Chapter 4. A Family Tradition

1. Liz Clarke, "Family Tradition," *The Washington Post*, February 12, 1999, p. D3.
2. Angus Phillips, "NASCAR's Rough Rider," *The Washington Post*, June 14, 1987, C6.
3. Ibid.
4. Ibid.
5. Rick Minter, "Determined Dirt-Track Racer Never Backed Off on Asphalt—or Forgot His Roots Off It," *The Atlanta Journal-Constitution*, February 21, 2001, p. B2.
6. Phillips, p. C6.
7. Ibid.

Chapter 5. From the Beginning

1. Bob Myers, "Dale Earnhardt, Jr. Q&A," *Circle Track,* April 27, 1998, p. 12.

2. Ibid.

3. Ibid.

4. Ibid.

5. David Poole, "The Son Also Rises," *The Charlotte Observer*, April 5, 1998, p. C3.

6. Myers, p. .

7. News services, "Earnhardt, Jr. Draws Comparisons to Gordon," *The Charlotte Observer*, April 16, 1998, p. C5.

Chapter 6. Phenom!

1. David Poole and Jim Utter, "For Earnhardt, Jr., Moment's Arrived for Distractions to Fade," *The Charlotte Observer,* May 30, 1999, p. C4.

2. Ibid.

3. David Poole, "J. Burton Joins Bonus Babies, Holds on for Victory in 600," *The Charlotte Observer,* May 31, 1999, p. C1.

4. "Dale Earnhardt, Jr. Drives to First Winston Cup Victory," *The Dallas Morning News*, April 2, 2000, p. 48.

5. Ibid.

6. Mark Zeske, "Here Comes the Son," *The Dallas Morning News*, February 7, 1999, p. 56.

Chapter 7. Tragedy on the Last Lap

1. David Poole, Tom Sorensen and Jim Utter, "Flag to Flag, a Race Driver's Final Day," *The Charlotte Observer*, February 20, 2001, p. C1.

2. Ibid.

3. Ibid.

4. Scott Fowler, "Dale Earnhardt—In an Instant, We Carolinians Lose One of Our Own," *The Charlotte Observer*, February 19, 2001, p. C1.

Chapter 8. Superstar on the Rise

1. Ken Garfield, "Earnhardt, Jr. Reflects on Faith, His Father on 700 Club," *The Charlotte Observer*, March 22, 2001, p. C3.

2. David Poole, "Grab a Seat, Take Wild Ride— IMAX Experience Takes You to NASCAR," *The Charlotte Observer,* March 9, 2004, p. C6.

3. David Poole, "Earnhardt, Jr. Has His Own Ideas," *The Charlotte Observer*, January 22, 2004, p. C4.

4. *Larry King Live*, CNN, Interview with Dale Earnhardt, Jr. and Jeff Gordon, February 23, 2004.

5. David Poole, "Earnhardt, Jr. Sweeps 1st Cup Win at Bristol," *The Charlotte Observer*, August 29, 2004, p. C1.

6. "Homestead: Dale Earnhardt, Jr. Race Report," *Motorsport.com*, November 21, 2004, <http://www.motorsport.com/news/article.asp?ID=173 922&FS=NASCAR-CUP> (December 20, 2004).

CAREER STATISTICS

Season	Races	Wins	Top 10s	Earnings	Final Standings
1999	5	0	1	$162,095	48
2000	34	2	4	$2,583,075	16
2001	36	3	15	$5,827,542	8
2002	36	2	16	$4,970,034	11
2003	36	2	21	$6,880,807	3
2004	36	6	21	$7,201,380	5
Totals	183	15	78	$27,624,933	n/a

WHERE
TO WRITE

Club E Jr.
P.O. Box 5190
Concord, N.C. 28027

INTERNET ADDRESSES

The Official Site of Dale Earnhardt, Jr.

http://www.dalejr.com

NASCAR.com

http://www.nascar.com

INDEX